Origami Bonsai

Origami Bonsai

Create Beautiful Botanical Sculptures From Paper

BENJAMIN JOHN COLEMAN

TUTTLE Publishing

Tokyo | Rutland, Vermont | Singapore

Acknowledgments

I would like to thank everyone who made this book possible, especially my parents for proofreading, and my niece Helen for confirming the folding diagrams.

Published by Tuttle Publishing, an imprint of Periplus Editions (HK) Ltd.

www.tuttlepublishing.com

Library of Congress Cataloging-in-Publication Data

Coleman, Benjamin John.
 Origami bonsai : create beautiful botanical sculptures from paper /
Benjamin John Coleman.
    p. cm.
 ISBN 978-0-8048-4103-0 (hardcover)
1. Origami. 2. Flowers in art. I. Title.
 TT870.C6164 2010
 736'.982--dc22

                              2009046050

ISBN: 978-0-8048-4103-0

DISTRIBUTED BY

North America, Latin America & Europe
Tuttle Publishing
364 Innovation Drive
North Clarendon, VT 05759-9436 U.S.A.
Tel: 1 (802) 773-8930; Fax: 1 (802) 773-6993
info@tuttlepublishing.com
www.tuttlepublishing.com

Japan
Tuttle Publishing
Yaekari Building, 3rd Floor
5-4-12 Osaki
Shinagawa-ku
Tokyo 141 0032
Tel: (81) 3 5437-0171; Fax: (81) 3 5437-0755
sales@tuttle.co.jp
www.tuttle.co.jp

Asia Pacific
Berkeley Books Pte. Ltd.
61 Tai Seng Avenue #02-12
Singapore 534167
Tel: (65) 6280-1330; Fax: (65) 6280-6290
inquiries@periplus.com.sg
www.periplus.com

First edition
14 13 12 11   5 4 3 2   1104EP

Printed in Hong Kong

Page 1: *The flowers and leaves of this sculpture are those from this book. The stems, branches and planter are made from paper, and showcase an advanced technique of mine that is not covered in this book.*

CONTENTS

This beautiful Origami Bonsai Geranium has multiple leaf and flower sizes for heightened realism.

The Tools of the Trade

Your life is about to change. You are about to enter a world where flowers with dramatic color distract with jaw-dropping intensity, and gardens cause drivers to jump out of their cars, cameras in hand, to photo-document the scene. After completing only a few projects, the way you view the world will change. You will start asking questions of Mother Nature. How did she combine those colors? Why does that species of bush create such twisting branches? A new sense of peace will develop in you, as the meditative aspects of this art form calm you. You will learn that there is nothing more relaxing after a busy day than to start a new Origami Bonsai project.

The potential of this art form is limitless. Every Origami Bonsai is unique because every twig is unique, but that's just the beginning. Origami Bonsai can be combined to create indoor gardens; they can be hung on the wall, placed over pictures and frames, combined with vases, furniture and other art. One of the most dramatic uses of Origami Bonsai is to combine them with lighting. When lit from below they create long, dramatic shadows. From across a room you can increase a piece's depth. Once you have assembled a few trees, and combined them with your existing décor, you will feel a new relationship develop between you and your living space. Like plants, Origami Bonsai make us feel more at home, more alive, but unlike plants, we feel a special affinity for them because they are our creations.

All that is required to complete the first project is one piece of 8 ½ by 11 paper, a pair of scissors and glue. You can find interesting paper at any stationery store, but for the best results you should use inexpensive, 20-pound white paper. I find that inkjet paper works best. It absorbs paint more evenly than photocopier or laser printer paper, and it "takes" folds with little damage.

Creating Origami Bonsai can become a team effort. Among partners, typically one will become a paint and color expert (type B personality) while the other becomes a folding fanatic (type A). These projects are cooperation-intensive, team-building, and uniting.

Tools of Professional Origami Bonsai

Let me be clear here, you don't need any of this stuff. And you shouldn't go on a shopping spree for your new hobby until you have assembled at least one Bonsai. Upon completion of a tree, you will feel a sense of satisfaction, a pounding in your chest, and a little rush of adrenalin. Once you have experienced these sensations, then by all means, go nuts, because the total here should come to well below $100.

 Tip: Discount stores sell 24 water color or acrylic paints for around $5 and a set of five good brushes for around $4.

From the Office Supply Store:
Paper—Buy a ream of 20 lb bond ink-jet paper.

Paper Cutter—Purchase a small rotary paper cutter from an office supply store.

From the Hardware Store:
Cutting Board—Purchase a new large cutting board made from wood. Make sure it has at least one flat side (many have grooves cut into them to drain juices).

Wall Paper Seam Roller—Purchase a wallpaper seam roller that has a wooden roller, and preferably a wooden handle as well. Do not purchase a seam roller that has a metal roller, as you will damage your cutting board.

Adjustable Clamp—You'll need a clamp to hold your work temporarily. I like the new-fangled type, which has a lever grip, like a calking gun, to adjust.

Origami Bonsai sculptures add a bit of color and beauty to any part of the home.

From the Craft Store:

Glue Gun—Get a high temperature or dual temperature glue gun. Leave the dual temperature glue gun set to "high."

Glue Sticks—Buy a bag of high temperature glue sticks. They're hard to find, but they are less "stringy" than the low temperature ones.

Glue Dipping Bowl—This is a circular bowl that heats up and melts the glue. It allows you to dip leaf stems into the bowl rather than juggling a hot glue gun and a bunch of leaves.

From the Drug Store:

Magnification Glasses—Get the greatest magnification you are comfortable with, even if your eyesight is good. These glasses will help you attain professional results when cutting paper, working with tiny flowers, etc.

From the Art Store:

Paintbrushes—Purchase a set of paintbrushes for watercolors. They should have medium-soft bristles.

Watercolor Paint—You need a set of watercolors. You can use sets designed for children for experimenting,

but as soon as you attempt a real project, purchase watercolors that come in "toothpaste tubes."

Artists' Medium—Get a tub of Artists' Medium. This seems only to be sold at art stores, so you may need to make a special trip or search the Internet. I use "matte" Artists' Medium.

Acrylic Paint—I use very limited amounts of acrylic paint for special effects. I don't like acrylics because they never seem to dry completely and leave paper feeling like shower curtain material. They also smell horrible. Make sure you pick up Gold and Silver, as we'll use these for the "silk-technique" (page 38).

From the Market:

Paint Cups—There's no need to buy paint cups as many products you purchase come packaged in them. Asian food comes with plastic dishes of sauce. These dishes work well. Granola that comes with yogurt is packaged in one of the best painting cups I've ever found. And some drink mixes come with individually packed cups.

Chopsticks—Chopsticks are useful for holding paper down while you paint. I rely on them, especially for working with smaller flowers.

The Project Folding Symbols

Writing an origami book presents many challenges, but there is one challenge that surpasses them all: books are two-dimensional, and Origami Bonsai is three-dimensional. In other words, the paper you are reading right now has essentially two dimensions, length and width. The flower you want to make has three dimensions, length, width, and height. How do I convey a three-dimensional subject when I only have two dimensions to work with?

I need ways to convey the third dimension when necessary. You will see the folding symbols presented in this chapter repeatedly throughout this book. On more complex subjects, you will not only see these symbols, but pictures with symbols as well. I have tried to diligently create folding diagrams that are easy to read, and ensure your success.

You may not fold the perfect flower the first time. You might even get stuck. But be patient, and approach Origami Bonsai as if it were a puzzle to be solved. The solution is here on the pages, but sometimes it's a good idea to put down the book and pick it up again in the morning.

You'd be surprised how many Origami models I've had to ponder overnight only to discover a simple resolution the following morning.

The folding demonstrations on the included DVD are an excellent reference as well.

This beautiful Origami Bonsai Columbine has multiple leaf and flower sizes for heightened realism.

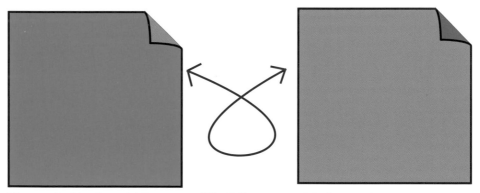

The symbol in the middle means "flip." The green side facing down now faces up after the flip symbol.

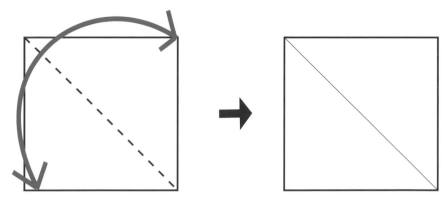

The double-ended arrow is my fold, and then unfold symbol. In this case it means you should fold the square diagonally, forming a triangle, and then unfold it.

Notice how the fold has become a thinner line in the square on the right. Also notice that the edges of paper are always a thick line.

Remember, previous folds are a thin line and paper edges are a thick line.

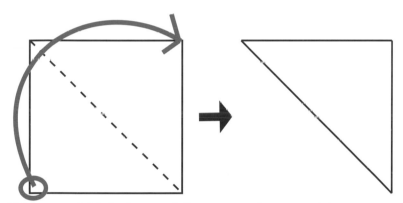

This means fold the bottom left corner to the upper right corner and leave it there.

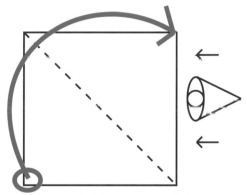

This means fold the bottom left corner to the upper right corner while watching the alignment on the right carefully, and leave it there.

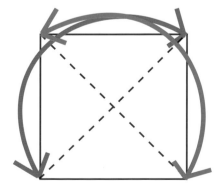

This means fold the square diagonally, from lower left to upper right, forming a triangle, and then unfold it, and then fold the square diagonally from lower right to upper left and unfold it.

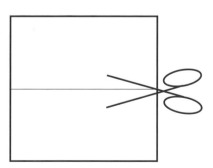

This means cut the thin line with scissors. In this case the paper will be cut in half forming two rectangles.

A Three-Dimensional Collapse

So far I've only presented folding symbols in two dimensions. Yellow folding symbols indicate movement in the third dimension. This is how we "collapse" a square into a more complex square one quarter its original size.

Each yellow dot will follow a yellow arrow to the center of the piece of paper.

Notice that the tips of the longer diagonal folds are migrating upward and toward the center, while the shorter horizontal and vertical folds are migrating to form the sides.

Now, all four corners (marked by yellow dots) are in the center of the square. The collapse is complete.

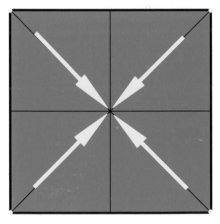

This is what the original folding diagram for a collapse will look like. Whenever you see a yellow arrow it means you lift its associated point up.

Reversing the Direction of a Fold

Whenever you see a red line, it means to reverse the direction of the existing fold under that line. Sharp, clearly-defined folds are easy to reverse. Dull, obscure folds are virtually impossible to reverse. You need a tool to sharpen your folds. If you do not have a wallpaper roller, you can use your fingernail to sharpen folds, but a better alternative is to use a wooden paint-mixing stick, a plastic putty knife, or a plastic spatula. Do not use metal tools, as you could rip your paper. Use of anything other than a wallpaper roller may damage your paper's painted surface.

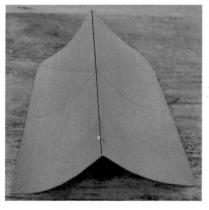

Virtually all folds depicted in this book are "valley" folds.

Depicted above is a "mountain" fold. In other words its sides slope up. The red line means we need to make it a "valley" fold, or make its sides slope down. This is done by flattening the adjacent paper areas and sliding a finger under the fold in the new direction desired.

This is how it will look after completing the reverse fold. Notice that the original fold is now a "valley" fold. Remember, a red line on an existing fold means to reverse its direction. It does not always mean to reverse it from a mountain to a valley fold; the situation might require a valley fold to become a mountain fold.

Performing a Book Fold

A book fold is almost always required at some point following a collapse. A book fold mimics turning the pages of a book.

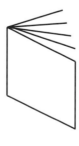

Our collapsed square from the *Three-Dimensional Collapse* section on the opposite page is being book-folded in these images.

The book fold is complete when the model has been flipped and the folding has been performed on both sides.

CHAPTER 2

Folding Leaves and Impatiens

At first glance a leaf seems to be a simple thing, however many plant species produce leaves of complex points and curves. Sometimes it is hard to get a square piece of paper to conform to these natural designs. After all, we're taking a two-dimensional piece of paper, with four corners, and "convincing it," through origami, to mimic natural species that have depth and multiple points. I have developed three basic leaf forms, standard, thin and oval, and a multitude of variations of these models.

The first leaf we'll explore is my "standard" leaf. I consider it the most beautiful when folded in small sizes. You'll find that the smaller you make these leaves, the more delicate and interesting they are.

Next I'll show you how to fold Impatiens. As with leaves, you will find that Impatiens appear much more interesting the smaller they're folded. If you had little or no trouble folding a leaf, you may wish to consider folding Impatiens for your first project at one quarter of the size I depict in these instructions. You may also want to skip ahead to Chapter 4, "Painting Leaves and Flowers," if you would like to produce a colored tree.

You don't need to paint your first Origami Bonsai. Even an unpainted, basic assembly like this one blends well with a woodland environment.

Folding a Leaf (Fold on Dotted Lines)

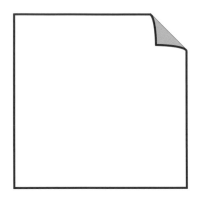

1. Start with the leaf color facing down.

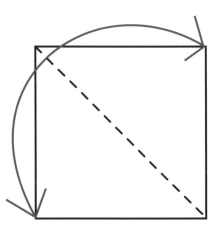

2. Fold, then unfold diagonally in half.

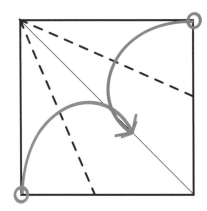

3. Fold the two corners to the center fold.

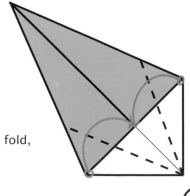

4. Fold the two corners to the center fold, and then flip.

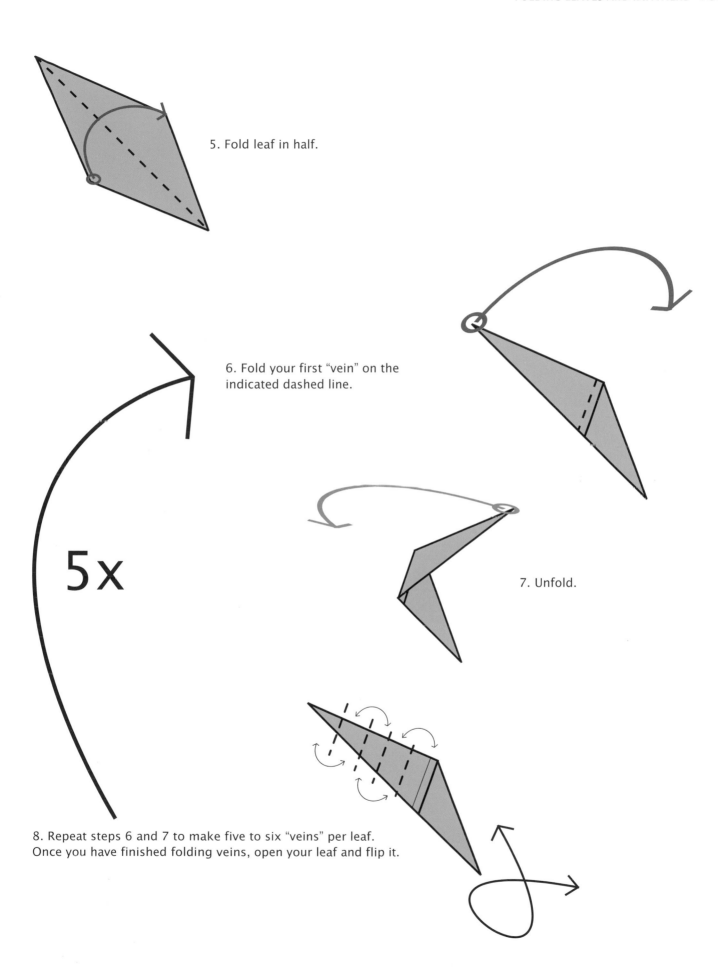

5. Fold leaf in half.

6. Fold your first "vein" on the indicated dashed line.

7. Unfold.

5x

8. Repeat steps 6 and 7 to make five to six "veins" per leaf. Once you have finished folding veins, open your leaf and flip it.

9. Fold the bottom corner up.

10. Now fold it down, leaving a small gap.

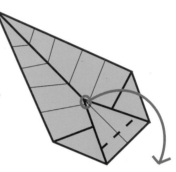

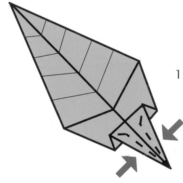

11. Narrow the stem by squeezing or pinching it.

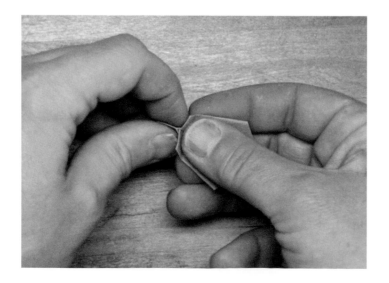

12. "Crimp" your leaf by holding the stem between the thumb and index finger of your left hand as you press with your right thumb. Notice that my fingernail does not touch the paper. This technique works only with smaller leaf sizes. Larger leaf stems must be narrowed by folding.

Mass Producing Squares

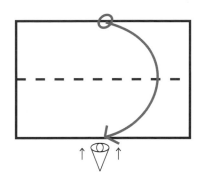

1. Fold a size A4 sheet of paper in half lengthwise. Align the bottom edges carefully.

2. Fold the bottom corners of the upper ply to the top. Align the top edges carefully. Flip it.

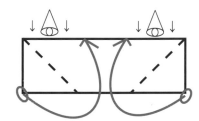

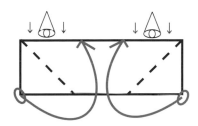

3. Repeat step 2 on this side.

4. Cut out the middle section and discard. Unfold one of the triangles.

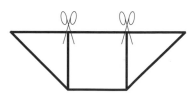

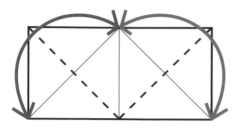

5. Fold, and then unfold the bottom corners to the top mid-point. Flip it.

6. Fold, and then unfold in half horizontally.

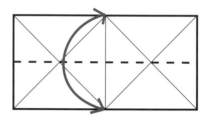

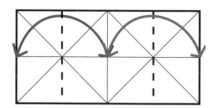

7. Fold and then unfold each vertical side to the center fold. This sheet is now ready to be painted with leaf color on the opposite side (this side is for flower color).

Cut in this pattern to make eight individual squares for leaves.

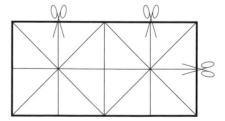

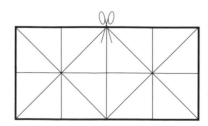

Cut in half to make flowers.

Folding Impatiens

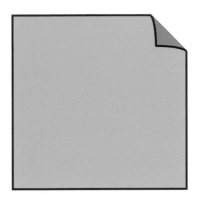

1. Start with the leaf color up, flower color down.

2. Fold and unfold diagonally in half in both directions. Flip it.

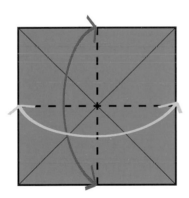

3. Fold and unfold horizontally and vertically in half.

4. Collapse the square, allowing the diagonal folds to collect in the center, and horizontal folds on the outside. Orient it with the open end pointing up.

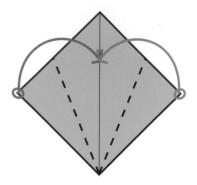

5. Fold left and right corners to the center aligned with the center fold.

6. Fold "tabs." Fold the inside corners out, aligned with the sides. Flip your model and repeat step 5 and 6 on the other side.

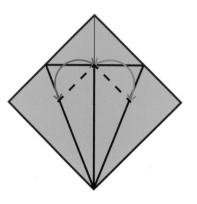

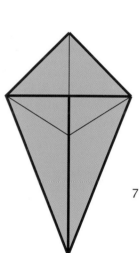

7. Your model should look like this.

8. Open your model completely. With the flower color up, reverse the direction of all folds colored red, so they will collapse correctly.

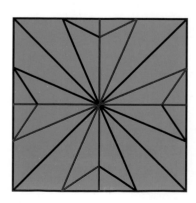

9. Your paper looks like this after reversing the longest folds. Now reverse the shorter "tab" folds.

10. This is how your Impatiens will look with the tabs folded in the proper direction.

11. Hold the bottom tip of the Impatiens with your thumb and index finger while bending each of the petals away from the center.

12. Shape the petals by bending them down. Your completed Impatiens should look like this.

Fine-Tuning Impatiens

You can use a spray bottle to help shape your Impatiens. Spray a very small amount of water on the Impatiens (you should not see drops of water, just a mist). Wait until the paper absorbs the water and begins to droop. Shape the petals to your liking and let the Impatiens dry. It will retain the shape you gave it when it was damp.

Folding Impatiens is easy once you've figured it out. I use Impatiens wherever I need tiny bits of color. The Impatiens, when folded to very small sizes, can also be used to create "baby's breath," a plant commonly used in arrangements and corsages. When painted and shaped with water, they can be quite dramatic.

CHAPTER 3

Building a Basic Bonsai Assembly

Even though plants are a part of our daily lives, we seldom consider copying them. One key component of Origami Bonsai is the accurate portrayal of botanicals in terms of leaf position; angle, density and numbers. This subject is complex on paper, but simple in implementation.

Plants absorb sunlight to obtain energy. Mechanically, they act like solar panels do; aligning themselves in such a way that the surface area facing the sun is maximized. We don't overlap solar panels, and trees don't overlap their leaves. When you assemble an Origami Bonsai, try not to attach leaves overlapping each other, as this will diminish the accuracy, beauty and realism of your piece. Taken to extremes, a perfectly assembled branch would have no overlapping leaves, and cast a solid shadow, with no light peeking through.

The angle at which leaves are attached is extremely important. The assembly we will attempt in this chapter is a wall piece. Because of this, we assemble the leaves parallel to our work surface. Please review all the assembly pictures before you start your project. If you make a mistake, don't lose heart. I'll show you a way to re-align leaves post-assembly in Chapter 14, "Fixing Mistakes."

Please read the safety instructions in Chapter 15, "Housekeeping" before assembling your first Origami Bonsai.

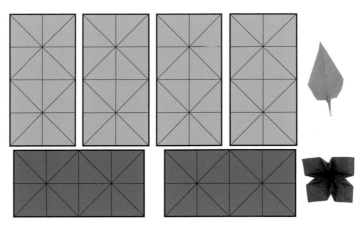

In this example, I prepared six rectangles. Four are larger, for the leaves, and two are smaller, for Impatiens. All six were painted green on one side, and the two smaller ones were painted blue on the other side.

1. Find a twig and trim it. Remove any branches that are brittle or thin.

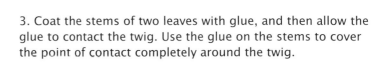

2. Apply glue with a hot glue gun.

3. Coat the stems of two leaves with glue, and then allow the glue to contact the twig. Use the glue on the stems to cover the point of contact completely around the twig.

4. Repeatedly attach pairs of leaves. Each pair should be approximately equally spaced, and aligned both to the twig and the previous pair.

Your twig should look like this. Note the symmetry, and that all the leaves have been attached parallel to the table's surface.

5. Apply a small amount of glue to the base of a flower.

6. Attach each flower between the stems of each pair of leaves.

These are two variations of Origami Bonsai using the same leaves and Impatiens. The one at left uses symmetry to attract the eye.

At right the twig is highlighted. It has Impatiens on the end of each twig segment, and leaves aligned in the direction of twig growth.

Tip: It is far easier to make an Origami Bonsai project fit a branch than it is to find a branch that fits an Origami Bonsai project.

Painting Leaves and Flowers

In this chapter I will describe how color can be used to create various special effects in your artwork. Depicted below is one of my more complex patterns. I have painted a circle of yellow on the smaller Primrose, and a set of filled curves on the larger one. When viewed from a distance, the color variation is not so noticeable. Instead, the yellow areas of the flower look deep, and the overall color becomes light yellow.

Obviously, Origami Bonsai flowers don't need to be this complex. However, as your Origami Bonsai expertise increases, you will want to push the creative envelope, developing more and more complex painting schemes for your creations. In terms of colors and shading, there are no limits.

One note of warning: real flowers have one attribute we can never reproduce—they're real. Often when I've attempted to mimic color schemes I've seen in nature, like lines of color, sudden transitions to a different color, or even something as simple as trying to combine yellow and blue on the same petal, I have failed miserably. Inevitably, blue mixes with yellow and creates green, and lines and arcs make the flower look "forced."

A yellow Columbine assembly before, and after, folding.

Be careful when investing time in painting. I urge you to try a scheme first, before starting a project with any more than five flowers. In my early days exploring this art form, I started many multi-flower projects that became disasters. Make some extra blank squares, then paint and fold prototypes of your color schemes prior to making the full investment in time.

When I first began this Origami Bonsai adventure, I vowed never to use orange. It is a difficult color to coordinate with. I never used it until I stumbled across some orange-pink Impatiens on a walk with my dog. Their color was striking enough to convince me to compose some pieces with orange-red, but I've been careful. My general rule for colors is, if it looks so good I'd like to eat it, then I've been successful.

You should be careful whenever you attempt to darken any of your colors with black. Don't underestimate this color. After ruining quite a few color schemes, I've learned to add it in microscopic amounts until I get my desired effect.

Don't forget that mixing colors can cause surprising results. For example, yellow and violet are great flower colors, but adding yellow to violet makes brown.

All of my project's paints are mixed individually, so I never exactly repeat any final color. And I don't save paint. I've found that it solidifies within a day or two and becomes unusable.

IMPORTANT:
All painting should be done on pre-folded sheets (after completing step 7 on page 22).

This is a selection of color schemes I've produced.

Painting Leaves with Variable Color

One component of Origami Bonsai is accurate portrayal. By folding veins, we simulate some of the texture of natural leaves; we need to increase this accuracy through painting. In this section, you will learn to paint a texture and a color onto your leaves simultaneously.

When we apply multiple coats of paint, some colors will mix, others will show through, and still others will appear thick. This variation in color makes your bonsai more appealing when viewed up close. The process of application is quite simple. I paint a thick layer of the primary color, with some artist medium mixed in, and then paint two more layers of the secondary color mixed much thinner.

I call the second and third coats of paint "wet coats," as I use a larger volume of this thinner mixture. I repeatedly brush back and forth in the longer direction of the sheet until it has absorbed all it will. Then I go back and forth repeatedly again, with a dry brush, to remove any excess paint that has not been absorbed. The paper becomes quite moist as these layers are worked in. When you apply these layers of paint, you will see your primary color start to vary throughout your sheet of leaves. I stop when I've got a finish that would make good wallpaper.

I selected these colors because they're easy for you to reproduce. But please, please, experiment with colors, because accurate portrayal is not the only component of Origami Bonsai. Creativity is just as important. Some of my most successful projects have come from colors I never thought would work.

Painting "Bamboo" Leaves

1. Start by painting a sheet with a mixture of yellow watercolor and artists' medium. This mixture should be fairly thick.

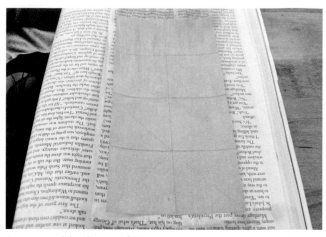

2. Now add a layer of dilute green watercolor and water with a small amount of artists' medium.

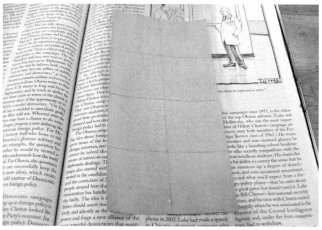

3. Finally, add one more layer of green watercolor and water with a small amount of artists' medium.

The result after folding.

Painting "Blue-Green" Leaves

To produce blue-green leaves start by painting one layer with a mixture of artists' medium, blue watercolor and water. Two layers of dilute artists' medium, green watercolor and water then follow this.

Painting "McIntosh" Leaves

To produce McIntosh leaves start by painting one layer with a mixture of artists' medium, red watercolor and water. Two layers of dilute artists' medium, green watercolor and water then follow this.

Painting Leaves with Gradient Color

Many plants appear to have gradient color leaves, especially in the fall. I have developed a technique for doing gradient color, for example, changing light green to bright red. I mix varying amounts of both colors with a white base to accomplish this.

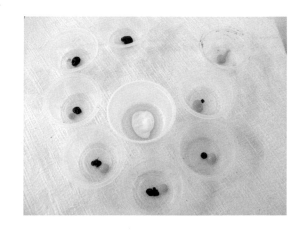

In this example I will do a gradient that goes from yellow to blue in eight steps, so I will paint eight or a multiple of eight, pieces of paper. I start by putting yellow watercolor in decreasing amounts in eight cups. I then add increasing amounts of blue watercolor.

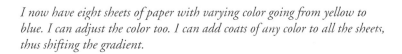
I add a mixture of water, white watercolor, and artists' medium to each cup. I then paint each sheet of paper with two coats of one cup's color.

I now have eight sheets of paper with varying color going from yellow to blue. I can adjust the color too. I can add coats of any color to all the sheets, thus shifting the gradient.

In this example, I painted all sheets with one coat of green, shifting the gradient to variations of green.

Painting Shading on Flowers

Obviously, flowers can be produced without shading, but you will find that shading adds color and increases the depth of your finished product. The "Bud," one of the variants of my flower-folding pattern, does not require shading. Most of my other designs benefit greatly from it.

IMPORTANT: Shades are always painted without artists' medium.
If you paint with medium, you'll get very little blending.

Four shading patterns are depicted here. They have been painted with a mixture of light blue watercolor and water.

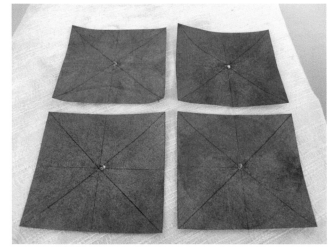

After applying two coats of ultramarine watercolor, artists' medium and water, the shaded areas appear fuzzy. This is key to successfully adding depth.

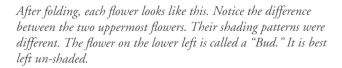

After folding, each flower looks like this. Notice the difference between the two uppermost flowers. Their shading patterns were different. The flower on the lower left is called a "Bud." It is best left un-shaded.

Flower Shading and Color

These primroses have been painted with circular shading. The shading was a mixture of ultramarine-blue watercolor and water. Then two coats of ultramarine-blue watercolor, water, and artists' medium were painted over the entire surface.

Shading: Blue watercolor and water.
Followed by: Two coats of a mixture of red watercolor, water and artists' medium.

Shading: Red watercolor and water.
Followed by: Two coats of a mixture of red watercolor, water and artists' medium.

Shading: Orange-yellow watercolor and water.
Followed by: Two coats of a mixture of yellow watercolor, water and artists' medium.

The Silk Technique

I have developed a process for combining acrylic silver and acrylic gold in my flower and leaf painting. I call this process the "silk technique," because of the reflective nature this coat of paint produces. My process is not limited to gold and silver, as I can add other colors to the acrylic mix as well. For example, when I do blue silk technique flowers, I add some acrylic blue to the silver mix.

It is important to note that you cannot use watercolors to achieve color effects with the silk technique. For some reason, when watercolors are combined with acrylic metallic, their color coats the surfaces of the tiny metallic bits, so the finished product is not very reflective.

Origami Bonsai Pin / Magnet
By Benagami

To be clear, I still paint the initial flower with watercolor and artists' medium. It's just the final coat of paint that is acrylic metallic, optional acrylic color, water, and artists' medium.

Make sure your leaf or flower paint has dried completely before performing the silk technique. If your paper is wet, leftover watercolor will bind to the metallic particles in the acrylic paint. The reflective properties of this technique will be greatly diminished.

 *Tip: When painted paper curls, it's dry.*

Two bamboo colored leaves are pictured above. The leaf on the right was finished with the silver silk technique. The leaf on the left was not. The silk technique leaf looks less colorful because it reflects more light.

This technique is just another of the tools of this craft. The choice is yours to use it or not.

Silk Technique Example

The silk technique adds both a shinier surface, and an improvement in color depth. Here's an example using multiple flower assemblies. Note how subtle the shading has become in the next picture on the following page.

This is a Columbine assembly. Shading has been painted in beige watercolor and water, followed by two coats of white watercolor, water, and artists' medium.

After the silk technique has been applied with a mixture of gold acrylic, water, and artists' medium.

Taken with the flash turned on, notice how light "dances" on the surface of the flower. The silk technique has added a visual complexity, with discreet shaded areas, and bright, light-reflecting curves. This is an example of a highly successful use of the silk technique.

Other Things

This art form is extremely flexible. The leaves of the tree above are made from digital images of a single side of a dollar bill. I call it a "Money Tree." It is on display in the CEO's office of Citizen's Bank in Providence, Rhode Island.

These are two clocks I've made. Clock movements are available in most craft stores.

Summary

Painting Leaves—Apply a mixture of water, watercolor, and artists' medium followed by two more diluted coats of a different color.

Shading Flowers—Choose a shading pattern based on the folding pattern you're going to use. The paint for your shade pattern is simply a mixture of water and watercolor. Then paint two coats of water, watercolor and artists' medium on top of that. Don't bother shading if you're going to use the "Bud" folding pattern.

Silk Technique—Make sure your paper has dried completely before performing the silk technique. You can tell when your paper is dry because it will begin to curl. To perform the silk technique, apply silver or gold acrylic optionally mixed with an acrylic color, water and artists' medium of a thin consistency.

Gradient Color—You can paint your leaves with gradient color to simulate changes in season. You can also combine gradient color with incremental leaf size changes to create other effects.

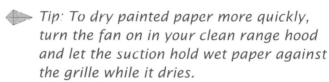

Tip: To dry painted paper more quickly, turn the fan on in your clean range hood and let the suction hold wet paper against the grille while it dries.

Pictured above is an example of gradient color from blue to yellow with a final coat of green.

CHAPTER 5

Finding Twigs and Stones

Long, meditative walks are a key component of Origami Bonsai. We have to develop a connection with nature, an eye for its beauty and complexity, and then combine this with our work, attempting not to duplicate, but to emulate what we have seen. It is important to realize that an effort to copy a plant will lead to frustration. We use plants as motivation and inspiration.

I spent some time trying to combine computer graphics with this art form. I took pictures of leaves, cut out their colors, and printed sheets of paper. The final product looked terrible. The colors seemed wrong, patterns never quite lined up, and I got nowhere. I attempted to do the same with flowers, only to fail again. Finally I realized, there was nothing wrong with the color, it was that the folding patterns lack the complexity required to duplicate the natural world. On a much more basic level, origami paper has four corners, real leaves and flowers have many corners.

Be observant as you walk. There's a lot going on around you. It's important to absorb as much as possible. For example, the blue flower pictured here is exquisite for a number of reasons.

Color: A pale blue with a white center.
Texture: The petals appear soft.
Symmetry: Five petals are highly symmetrical.

We can fold something similar, but it is unlikely we could duplicate this flower in origami. Our biggest impediment is that we only have four corners on a sheet of origami paper. It would be difficult to fold a flower that got around this limitation.

   We can use this flower as a model. We can duplicate the color using blue, violet, and white. We can also create a similar softness of texture in the application of paint, and use the standard Primrose folding pattern to simulate larger petals.

We can do more with the flower below. It has five petals as well, however one is largely hidden. We can achieve this color by mixing white, red and a small amount of blue. By folding this as an Impatiens, we'll obtain similar petals.

Finding Suitable Twigs

Tip: Use only dead branches as "green" branches age unpredictably and can warp, destroying an Origami Bonsai.

While an oak tree will make a strong bench, it won't make a strong Origami Bonsai branch. Over the past few years I have discovered some interesting properties of various species of plant. The most important, for our purposes, is long-term flexibility of twigs and branches.

   As many branches dry out, they become brittle, and fragile. Without flexibility, our projects become more and more delicate over time. A simple task, like moving an Origami Bonsai to clean behind it, can become a disaster, breaking branches, and destroying your work. I use dead, old growth mountain laurel branches because they maintain their elasticity over long periods of time.

   Both the picture on the bottom of the facing page and the picture to the lower-left are of a species of mountain laurel. These bushes produce twigs and branches of extreme beauty and flexibility. They have to, because they grow under other trees, in an ever-changing, sunlight-hungry environment. As Mountain Laurels grow, they have to reposition new growth to find sunlight as trees above them grow.

   Each year a Mountain Laurel will produce new twigs in an effort to find more sunlight. These twigs will sprout new leaves. Interestingly, the mountain laurel won't invest a lot in these new twigs unless they get additional sunlight. If the plant doesn't get additional light from the new twig, it doesn't continue in that direction, and tries a new one at the end of a more successful twig. Because of this, the twig that failed becomes brittle, and never grows a solid coat of bark.

   This makes brittle twigs easy to identify. Their outer-shell is different, with spots of a lighter-colored coating. I cut off all the brittle segments from every branch I use, because I've learned that failure to do so will result in a loss of many hours of work.

Mountain laurel is a member of the heath family, and is related to rhododendron and azalea. They are widely cultivated and grow in both temperate and tropical areas of the world. While this is the species I prefer for Origami Bonsai, I have made bonsai from oak, birch, blueberry, and many other varieties of plants.

The twig at right is made up of both new and old growth. Twig segments with pale bark need to be trimmed off, as they will become brittle with age.

This is the same branch with new growth segments removed. This can be used for Origami Bonsai.

Pictured at right is an example of healthy old-growth bark. This would make an excellent choice for Origami Bonsai.

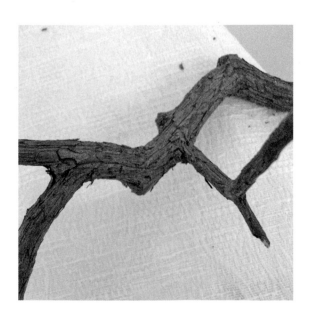

Finding Stones to Mount Origami Bonsai

Stones to mount Origami Bonsai are fairly easy to find. You can use any stone that has a porous or irregular surface. It's fun to try to match stone color to your work's color.

In recent years I have moved almost exclusively to using "clinkers," melted impurities in coal from furnaces, to mount my works. Clinkers can be found in any geographical area where coal was used for fuel. They are commonly dumped in piles in remote locations. They range from the size of pebbles to large rocks.

The advantage of clinkers is twofold. First, they are light, as air bubbles have been trapped inside the molten rock. Secondarily, they look like molten lava, and evoke visions of Asian volcanic activity.

If you plan to ship your bonsai, whether commercially or as gifts, its weight should be considered. Not only does it cost more to ship a heavier stone, but the greater the weight of your mount, the more potential energy it has. In other words, a heavier Origami Bonsai is more likely to sustain damage.

I used to ship the bonsai mount in a box separate from the tree to avoid damage. However this presented a problem, because the recipient would have to re-glue the piece, inevitably changing its perspective. I now use thin wires to tie my Origami Bonsai to the box.

I make holes in the box, and run multiple wire ties in and around twig segments, and around the stone. This, along with "this side up" arrows and "fragile" stickers has proven fairly successful.

Head outside for an abundant supply of mounting stones.

When shipping sculptures, make sure you tie the stone securely. I find that wire ties work well.

Wallpaper Roller Shortcuts

My wallpaper roller is an indispensible tool that increases the accuracy and crispness of my folds. It also allows me to make multiple folds through many sheets of paper simultaneously, thus increasing my productivity. I use it not only to fold, but also to flatten folds, like when I have to do reverse folds in Impatiens and flowers.

When I started doing lots of Origami Bonsai I used my index finger's nail to sharpen folds. My nail wore down to nothing very quickly. I then switched to a wooden paint-mixing stick for the same job, but it damaged the paper. I was shopping at the hardware store one day and discovered the wallpaper roller.

I've had the same roller for years now. Compared to rolling the seams of thousands of feet of wallpaper, this is an easy job, so it's held up well. I have often thought of buying another one, as a backup, but I don't see the point. This roller should last my lifetime, and a few more, as long as I take care of it.

I keep water away from my roller. Whenever I'm going to paint, I put my roller away. It never rolls on any surface other than paper or my cutting (folding) board. I never oil the roller's bearings, as they don't need it, and I don't need any oil contaminating my work. And I never, ever, attempt to roll a piece of paper that's still wet.

A wallpaper seam roller is fundamentally just a cylinder attached to a handle. They're typically available in hardware stores. This useful tool will greatly increase your accuracy, making folds sharper and easier to reverse.

To Fold Four Leaves at a Time

1. Instead of cutting your squares into leaf-sized ones, collapse them.

2. Roll the collapsed square's folds.

3. Fold the first half of the leaf, folding all four pleats of paper and roll the folds.

4. Fold the stem side of the leaf and roll again.

5. Open the paper and roll it flat, then cut.

6. You now have four pre-folded leaves!

Easier Flower Completion

1. As you'll see again in Step 9 in the following chapter, roll your roller on the two side folds.

2. Roll your paper flat before the collapse.

You can apply the same rolling technique to Impatiens. Whenever you need to do multiple reverse folds, rolling the original folds, then rolling them flat will save a lot of time.

Tip: A sharp fold easily reverses. Use your wallpaper roller to sharpen any fold before you attempt to reverse it.

Folding the Basic Flower Form

The basic flower form is a highly complex origami folding pattern. Its one advantage is that it is symmetrical. I would recommend approaching this as if it were a puzzle; one that you are unlikely to complete correctly on the first try, but will master after a few attempts. You should not attempt folding a flower until you have successfully completed folding a few examples of the Impatiens from Chapter 2, "Folding Leaves and Impatiens."

I stumbled upon this pattern by accident. I was quite sleepy, attempting to fold an animal, when I repeated some folds too many times. I noticed a beautiful symmetry developing and continued experimenting with my mistake. Over a period of months, I fine-tuned the pattern. Over a period of years I have developed numerous variations of the Basic Flower Form.

In illustrating this folding pattern, I have taken many photos. Some of the techniques are more complex, and required extra photos to document. Therefore, not every photo is a step.

I start with one piece of paper painted dark blue on the flower side and light green on the stem side.

Top right: *A plant with triple primrose flowers.*

Right: *This is what the Basic Flower Form looks like before it is folded into one of the many flower varieties it is capable of representing.*

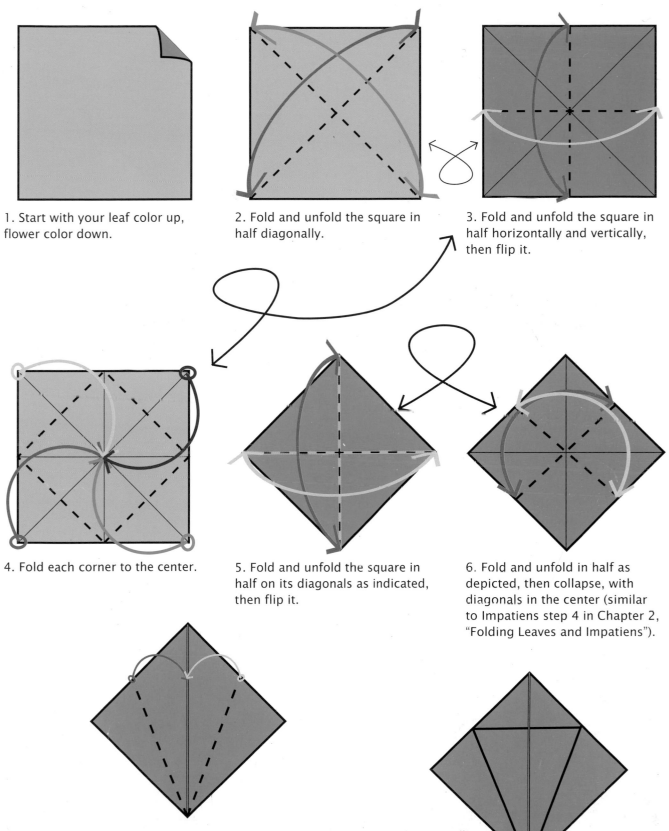

1. Start with your leaf color up, flower color down.

2. Fold and unfold the square in half diagonally.

3. Fold and unfold the square in half horizontally and vertically, then flip it.

4. Fold each corner to the center.

5. Fold and unfold the square in half on its diagonals as indicated, then flip it.

6. Fold and unfold in half as depicted, then collapse, with diagonals in the center (similar to Impatiens step 4 in Chapter 2, "Folding Leaves and Impatiens").

7. Diagram is larger than scale. Your model should be ¼ the size it was in step 6. With the open end at the top, fold the top two left and right corners to the center. Flip and do the same on the other side (similar to Impatiens step 6 in Chapter 2, "Folding Leaves and Impatiens").

8. Your model should look like this. Flip it and repeat step 6 on the opposite side.

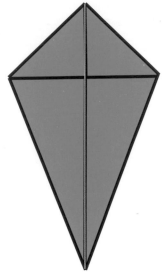

9. Your model should look like this.

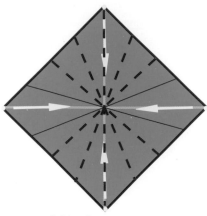

10. Unfold your model back to step 6. Orient as in step 5. Collapse such that the square's diagonals (yellow and green lines) end up in the center of the collapse. You will need to reverse fold all dashed red lines.

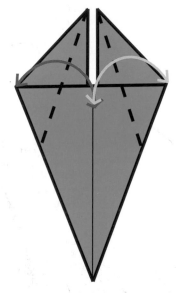

11. Fold and unfold left and right corners to the center.

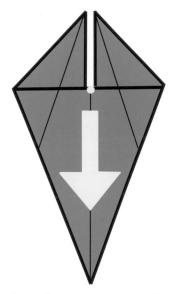

12. Pull the yellow point up and then squash it flat.

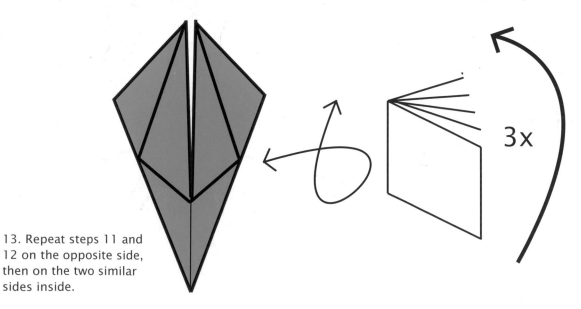

13. Repeat steps 11 and 12 on the opposite side, then on the two similar sides inside.

3x

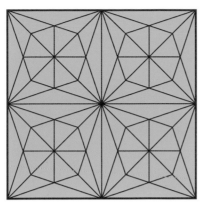

14. Completely unfold your model.
Your square will look like this. Push up from underneath at the center and squeeze the corners to collapse into the Basic Flower Form.

15. Continue collapsing.

 *Refer to the companion DVD for help if you run into any difficulty folding this form.*

16. The completed collapse. Now combine pairs of outer corners and fold flat.

The completed Basic Flower Form.

If you open the four petals, you will have a "Michelle I" flower.

 If your leaf and flower colors are on the wrong sides, your model was backwards at step 8.

Intermission

The following collection of photos shows some of my finished Origami Bonsai models, which are meant to inspire you as you prepare to delve into the second half of the book's content.

The images to the right and below show a bonsai I call "The Circle of Life." It is made of leaves and Impatiens using pre-printed origami paper. There are two frogs made from the same paper, a large one on the large base-leaf, and a small one on the leaf at the end of the twig. They are well camouflaged and very hard to see, as are frogs in nature. This is one of my earliest Origami Bonsai works.

This is one of my first works after discovering the basic flower form. It features thistle-style flowers. I hadn't yet discovered Artist Medium so the leaves have suffered the ravages of time.

This is a depth-enhanced Origami Bonsai with five leaf sizes and three flower sizes. Notice how it appears to "pop" out at you.

This is one of my first omni-directional Origami Bonsai, designed to be viewed from any angle.

This Origami Bonsai has Hyacinth blossoms in a wonderful shade of blue with dark green leaves.

This Origami Bonsai has five leaf and flower sizes, however its branch lacked the depth necessary for an "accurate deception." When combined with a ceramic piece with a similar depth deception ratio, the look is quite dramatic.

Subtlety of color makes this one of my favorites.

This is a bushy Origami Bonsai. The leaves have been attached to the twig in a dense configuration. It has eleven leaf sizes and five flower sizes folded in both Bud and Primrose style.

This is a similar Origami Bonsai with three leaf and flower sizes. A particularly nice piece because the twig bends in a 180 degree turn, thus allowing the bonsai to overhang its mount.

This Origami Bonsai has two distinct plant species. Both plants have leaves in five sizes and flowers in three.

This is the first depth-enhanced Origami Bonsai. It has leaves in five sizes and flowers in three sizes. It was assembled with the help of a laser alignment tool I no longer use.

Folding Other Leaf Varieties

Over the years I have developed a few different leaf shapes. My favorite is the leaf you have already learned to make, however I have also developed narrow leaves, oval leaves, and curly leaves. All my leaf designs are easy to learn.

Some leaves look very different in larger sizes. The two wide-curled leaves below are both of the same folding pattern, but look quite different when folded in large versus small sizes. You will find that the standard leaf looks quite mediocre in larger sizes, but if you add a curl, its look improves dramatically.

The most important tip I can offer is to make your leaf colors interesting. Paint your leaves with multiple coats of paint, allowing the color to vary throughout your work. It is this color variation that makes Origami Bonsai leaves most interesting.

These are some of the leaves I have developed for Origami Bonsai.

Folding Narrow Leaves

Narrow leaves add a little drama to anything you make. If you're not going to curl them, make sure you fold veins before doing the crimp fold.

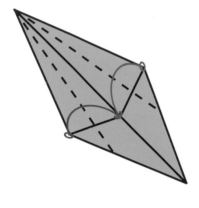

1. Starting from step 4 in "Folding a Leaf" on page 18, narrow the leaf by folding the sides to the center.

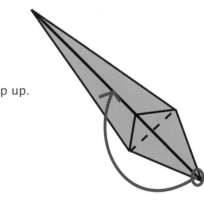

2. Fold the bottom tip up.

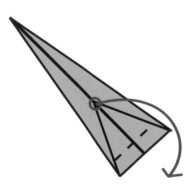

3. Fold the same tip back down, leaving a gap.

4. Squeeze the stem together with thumb and index finger, then "crimp," as in "Folding a Leaf" step 12 (page 20).

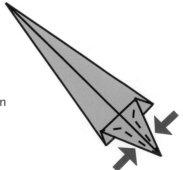

Folding Long Stem Leaves

Dramatic when attached to an Origami Bonsai in groups of three, the long stem leaf is a useful design.

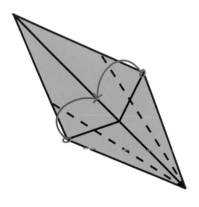

1. Starting from step 4 in "Folding a Leaf." Narrow the leaf by folding the sides to the center.

2. Fold the bottom tip up.

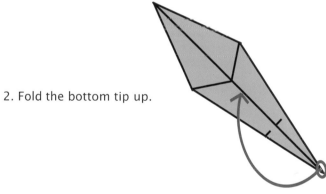

3. Fold the tip from step 2 back down leaving a gap as shown.

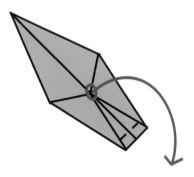

4. Squeeze the stem together with thumb and index finger, then "crimp," as in "Folding a Leaf" step 12 (page 20).

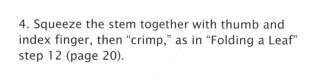

Folding Oval Leaves

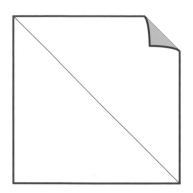

1. Start with a square, leaf color side down, folded in half diagonally.

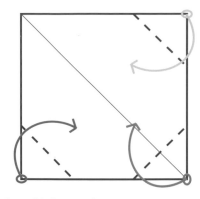

2. Fold three adjacent corners to a point midway between the center and the folded side.

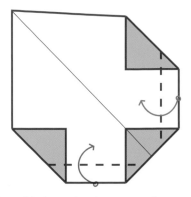

3. Fold the sides between the folds from step 2 towards the center.

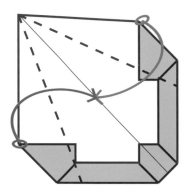

4. Fold the longest sides to the center fold.

5. Fold the top point to a point just beyond the center.

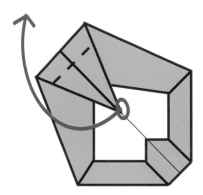

6. Fold the point back leaving a gap.

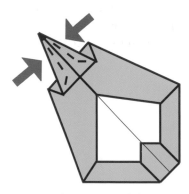

7. Narrow the stem and then crimp.

Oval leaves look best when painted on both sides.

Adding a Curl to Leaves

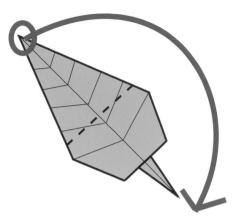

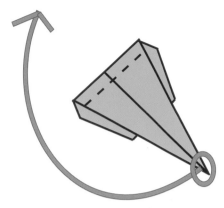

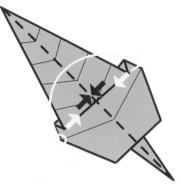

1. Start with any leaf variety, facing up. Fold the tip down, beyond the end of the stem.

2. Fold the tip back up leaving a gap.

3. Pick up the leaf. Pinch the fold on the underside while folding it in half.

4. Pinch bottom center while pulling down on tip and stem.

If you've performed the folds properly, the folds on the outside of the leaf should open, while the fold in the center of the leaf stays closed. This forces the paper to expand on the outer edge and creates a curl.

Narrow leaves look especially good when curled.

Curling a leaf requires patience and a bit of determination. Practice with an unpainted leaf first.

You can fold another curl closer to the end of the leaf following the same procedure. Curling leaves is not easy, however curled leaves can greatly enhance an Origami Bonsai either as the primary plant's leaves, or as a secondary shrub's leaves.

Finishing Variations of the Basic Flower Form

In this chapter I discuss various techniques for finishing the folds of the basic flower form. The picture above shows four varieties of flower you can produce. These flowers can be combined, which is discussed in the next chapter.

Determining which type of flower you will use is part of the planning stages of a project. Each flower has distinct attributes that can increase or decrease the appeal of your finished work. This decision should be made after you have found a suitable branch, because finding a branch for a specific flower can be time consuming.

For example, a Bud looks like a Bud from any direction. It is an extremely flexible flower, as it will be recognized even when seen from the back side.

The Primrose does not share this functionality; instead, it is only recognizable at small angles beyond straight in front of its audience. Finding a branch where most of the twig-ends face the viewer is significantly harder. If you love the Primrose, and want wide perspective in your finished work, take a look at the "Hyacinth" in Chapter 13, "Creating Multi-Flower Assemblies."

Top right: *Four Basic Flower Form variants.*

Left: *Mounts for Origami Bonsai are not limited to stones. Here I used a can of Coca-Cola as a mount.*

The "Primrose"

While you can vary the size of Primroses, you cannot vary the size of the hole in the center of the flower. It is not proportional, which is why smaller Primroses are more visually pleasing.

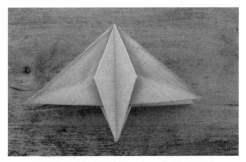

1. Start with the basic flower form from Chapter 7, "Folding the Basic Flower Form."

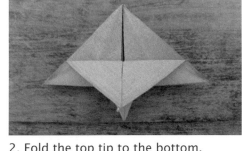

2. Fold the top tip to the bottom.

3. Now fold the same tip up to its fold. Repeat on the opposite side, then rotate petals and repeat on the inside.

4. Your model will look like this.

3x

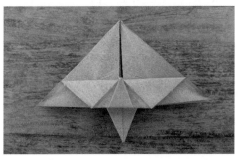

5. Now separate the petals, spacing them evenly.

6. Separate the sides of a petal while using your index finger to spread the middle of the petal out. Repeat this step for the other three petals.

Your completed primrose should look like this.

The "Thistle"

This variant has four corners protruding from the center. You can paint these corners, which turn out to be the sides of the original square of paper, a different color.

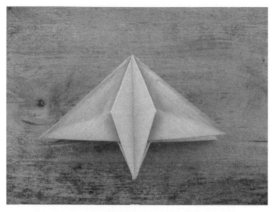

1. Start with the basic flower form from Chapter 7, "Folding the Basic Flower Form."

2. Fold the top tip to the bottom.

3. Now fold the same tip up to a point halfway between the previous fold and the top. Repeat on the opposite side, then rotate petals and repeat on the inside.

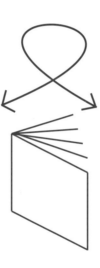

Follow the last four steps of the "Primrose" (Page 17). Your thistle should look like this.

The "Daisy"

The Daisy is an incredibly flexible flower. In the final steps, you can shape the petals, making them flat, concave, or bulged. This flower can be combined with quarter-sized flowers to produce many effects.

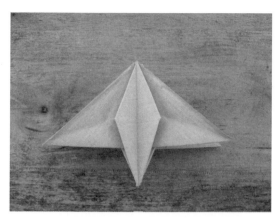

1. Start with the basic flower form from Chapter 7, "Folding the Basic Flower Form."

2. Fold the top tip down, following the folds on the petals, collapsing the tip in the center. Repeat this for all four petals.

3. Your flower should look like this. Open each petal from the top. Some of your flower color will end up on the bottom of each petal.

The completed Daisy.

Daisy Finish-Folding Options

Pull the petal tips to achieve a concave daisy look.

Pull petals down to get a droopy look.

The "Bud"

Buds are a flexible and beautiful variety of flower. One thing you may want to do is mix Buds and Primroses. This will give the impression that your Origami Bonsai is going through the transition from budding to blooming.

1. Start with the basic flower form from Chapter 7, "Folding the Basic Flower Form."

2. Fold the top tip to the bottom.

3. Fold the same tip up to its fold. Repeat on opposite side, then rotate petals and repeat on the inside.

4. Your model will look like this. Now separate the petals, spacing them evenly.

5. Open and spread two petals.

6. Squeeze the two petals in the center of the flower.

7. Push the petals up vertically from the inside. Repeat steps 5, 6, and 7 on the other two petals.

8. Your finished Bud should look like this.

CHAPTER 11

Incremental Leaf Sizes and Depth Enhancement

I first displayed an Origami Bonsai with incremental leaf size at an art show in Connecticut. I had three versions, one of which sold in the first couple of hours. People gathered around the pieces with different sized leaves, especially the one which sold quickly. The piece that sold quickly was different. Its leaf size increment was smaller, making it impossible to tell with your eyes that the leaf size varied.

After that show I made the prototype pictured below. It had very few leaves and high-contrast flowers. I made the leaves in five sizes and the flowers in three sizes. I assembled it using a laser alignment tool I made. I started with the smallest leaves, attaching them to the points of greatest depth in the piece. Because I couldn't afford a high-powered laser, I had to turn the lights off to mark each point on the twig that required a leaf.

While this project was the most time-consuming I have ever attempted, I learned a great deal. Most importantly, that the human eye can be fooled as long as there aren't visual references revealing the deception, or if the deception is discreet. In other words, I can make an Origami Bonsai look a little bit deeper than it actually is, but not a lot deeper.

I assemble variable leaf size Origami Bonsai with the largest leaves closest to the viewer, and the smallest leaves farthest away. I know I've successfully performed the deception if my audience can't tell the leaf size varies. I can measure the accuracy of my deception using light.

To do this, I turn the Origami Bonsai around, so that the leaves and flowers face a wall. Then I point a single light source at the sculpture from across the room. The shadows of all the leaves should appear to be exactly the same size. That's because the smallest leaves are closest to the light source, casting a larger shadow, than the larger leaves farther from the light source.

If you don't understand, then try it. Make two leaves of different sizes. Hold them below a single light bulb, one in each hand, and move them up and down until they cast the same size shadow. Make note of the distance. Now hold them in front of you at a distance of eight inches (20 cm) or more. Hold the smaller leaf closer, and move it until it completely blocks your view of the larger leaf. You will find that the distance between the two leaves is the same in both demonstrations. I call this the "gap" between leaf sizes.

I vary leaf size because it makes my finished product more interesting and marketable.

In this picture, two squares appear to be the same size. There is no visual reference to distance.

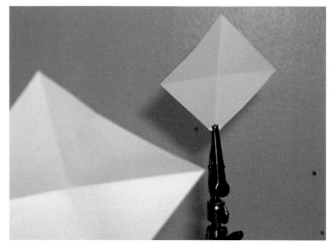

In this picture, one square seems to be very distant from the other. Again, there is no visual reference to distance.

In fact, these squares are separated by about five inches (13 cm). One square is approximately $^1/_8$ of an inch (3 mm) shorter on each side than the other.

This Origami Bonsai has leaves that vary in both size and shade. Smaller leaves, attached deeper in the piece, were shaded with more blue than closer leaves. This enhances the effect, but adds a lot more time to the painting process.

The Origami Bonsai above has eleven leaf sizes and five flower sizes (also pictured at the top of page 61).

Producing Incrementally Sized Leaves and Flowers

1. Fold a size A4 piece of paper. Leave a ⅛ inch (3 mm) gap.

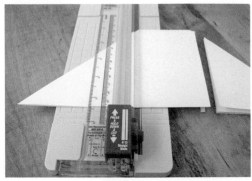

2. Fold each corner to the center fold (see Page 21). Cut the middle out.

3. Before you discard the middle, tear off the thin pieces on the left and right. They represent your "step."

4. The two pieces from step 3 define the new sheet's gap. Fold your next sheet, leaving this distance at the top.

5. For the next increment, use one of your "step" pieces along with one of the previous sheet's to gap the next piece of paper.

Notice, I use one "step" piece and the previous sheet's leftover to form the gap of a new sheet.

Here I have cut 5 incremental leaf sizes.

6. In pencil, identify each size with a number on the flower side of the sheet (diagonal folds pointing up).

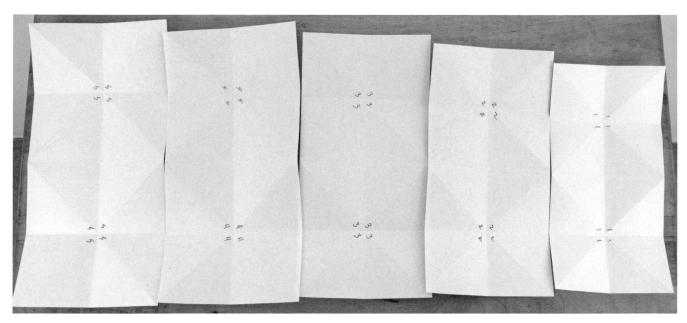

7. If you fold one more sheet in half, you will end up with five leaf sizes. Before I paint, I put a number on each leaf representing its size. If you put the numbers in the center, with the diagonal folds pointing up, they will be hidden after you fold the leaves. You'll still be able to peek at the numbers by pulling the folds back. This is useful, especially when you use a smaller step.

8. If you plan to make flowers as well, produce an extra sheet for each size. In this picture I've produced five sheets for leaves and three for columbine flower assemblies. When making paper for flower assemblies, I often letter, rather than number, so I don't confuse flowers with leaves.

Creating a Sorting Tray

Once you've prepared a set of incrementally sized leaves, you'll need to have something to put them in. Here's how to make an Origami Sorting Tray.

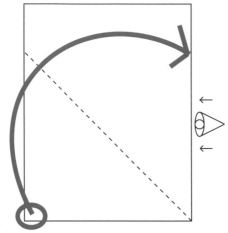

1. Start with a size A4 sheet of paper. Fold it diagonally, aligning the right edges of the paper.

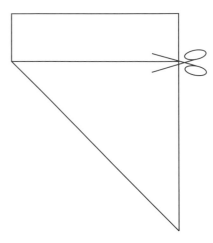

2. Cut the upper portion of the paper to create a triangle, and open it to get a square.

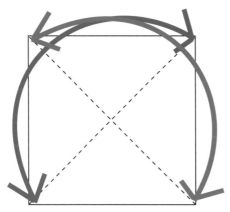

3. Fold diagonally in both directions and unfold.

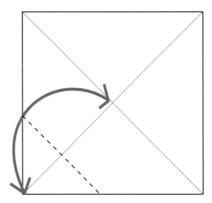

4. Fold one corner to the center and unfold.

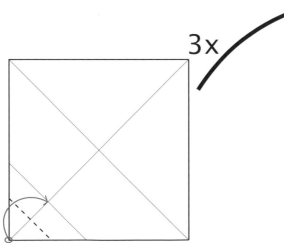

5. Fold the corner to the fold you just made. Repeat for all four corners.

3x

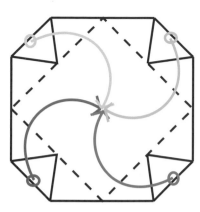

6. Now fold all four sides to the middle.

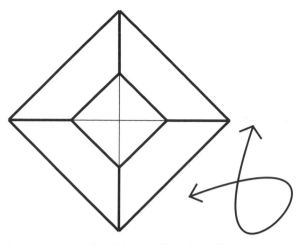

7. Your paper should look like this. Flip your model.

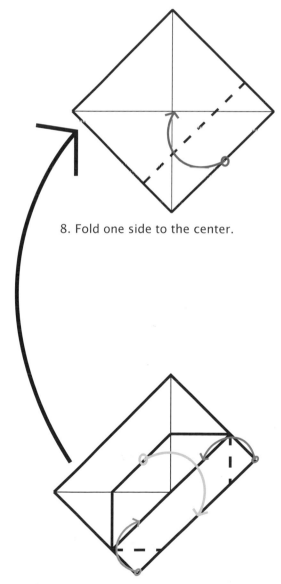

8. Fold one side to the center.

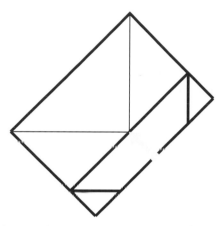

9. Lift the top flap of the side you just folded up and open it.

10. Fold the corners of the lowest tier to the center fold and close the flap. Repeat steps 8 and 9 on the other side.

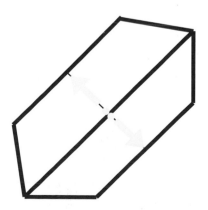

11. Pull the top layers up.

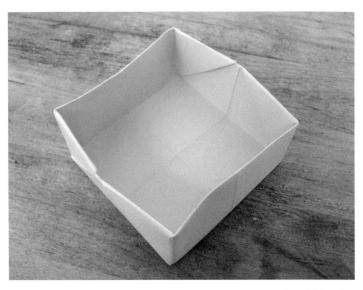

Vary the size of your boxes by starting with smaller squares. If you want to make a box top, start by making your box from a square slightly smaller than the square for the top.

12. Shape the box, and sharpen its corners. It should look like this when complete.

Origami boxes are quite versatile. I make gift boxes with them for lapel pins and other small items. I've also glued boxes together in a row and used them as a sorting box, or glued origami animals in them to depict little stories.

Boxes can be combined with leaves and flowers to create neat sculptures.

Take Origami Bonsai with You

You can put your unfolded leaves and flowers in take-out containers. This makes them portable, allowing you to fold anytime and anywhere. I often fold in waiting rooms, and when traveling. I've even folded while sailing on a schooner in Penobscot Bay, Maine.

I also own a large tackle box that contains four, compartmentalized sub-boxes. These are fantastic for transporting large projects.

The tackle box above contains the leaves for a large project.

CHAPTER 12

Assembly of a Depth-enhanced Origami Bonsai

I will now show you how I assembled a depth-enhanced Origami Bonsai. This bonsai has five incrementally-sized gradient color leaves and three flowers. At first glance this seems intimidating, but broken down into steps it becomes quite easy.

Before you begin an incrementally-sized-leaf Origami Bonsai assembly you need to determine maximum and incremental depth. It's important to remember that you will assemble the bonsai with the largest leaves shallowest (closest to the viewer), and the smallest leaves deepest (furthest from the viewer). Leaves are attached in layers, from smallest to largest.

An origami hummingbird feasts on an Origami Bonsai Hyacinth flower.

5   4   3   2   1

Depth enhancement depends upon the perspective of the viewer.

Determining Maximum Depth

Hold your largest leaf in one hand, and smallest in the other at least eight inches (20 cm) away from your eyes. Move the largest leaf away until it appears to be the same size as the smallest. This is your maximum depth. The branch you have selected for this project should be no deeper than this measurement. If you attempt to use a branch with greater depth, this illusion will be revealed.

Determining Incremental Depth

Incremental depth is the difference in depth between two sequentially-sized leaves. We determine this depth using the same technique described previously. This is the distance between layers of leaves.

Example

As the incremental size variation decreases, "fudge" factor increases. In other words, you could make all your leaves the same size (zero increment), in which case it doesn't matter how shallowly or deeply you attach any leaves. As your increment gets larger, it gets harder to hide the change in size.

2　　　　1

The example above shows an Origami Bonsai with two increments in leaf size. In the picture on the right you can see that the leaves and flowers have been installed in two distinct planes (the planes are highlighted in gray), at a fixed distance from each other. You can also see that there is a large variation in leaf and flower size between the two planes, something that is not apparent in the left-hand picture. In the picture on the left, the deeper leaves and flowers just look distant, not smaller.

The incremental depth of this Origami Bonsai is six inches (15 cm). Its maximum depth is also six inches because there are only two leaf sizes. If there were a third size, incrementally equal between the two existing sizes, then there would be another layer of leaves between the two you see in the picture on the right. I chose this branch because it illustrates this illusion with only two sizes of leaf.

1. Trim a branch removing all of the current year's growth. I've trimmed the branch tips so I can use the same size flower on each one.

2. Fit the twig on a stone or other suitable material.

3. Remove bark from the area that will be glued to the stone.

4. Apply hot-glue and hold together until the glue cools.

5. Sand former branch connections so your twig will appear to have grown into its new configuration (these areas will be painted later).

6. Look at both the perspective and profile views of your twig. You need to:

- **Determine the number of flowers you will need.** I'm going to use three Columbine assemblies, one flower on each branch tip. All three flowers can be the same size.
- **Estimate the number of leaves you will need.** I will cut five incremental sheets for a total of 40 leaves.
- **Decide how big your step should be.** This is based on the depth of the piece. For this Bonsai I will prepare paper for five incremental leaf sizes with a small step.
- **Consider leaf color.**

7. Cut leaf and flower sheets based on the information you obtained in step 6.

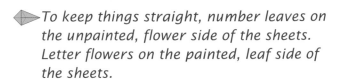*To keep things straight, number leaves on the unpainted, flower side of the sheets. Letter flowers on the painted, leaf side of the sheets.*

8. Paint leaf color on the five rectangles you will use for leaves. Also paint your leaf color on the areas that will be visible on flowers. I used a blackened-yellow gradient with a green base and a silk technique final coat of light green.

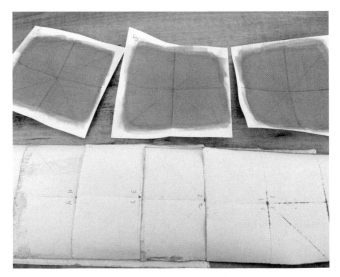

9. Number leaf sheets according to size on their un-painted backs, in the center of each square. By doing this, if you get confused at any point, you can open the tip of the leaf to confirm the size.

I start with the smallest, darkest leaves. Here the small-dark leaves are numbered with 1s, the largest with 5s.

10. It is now time to consider flower color. The leaf color combination I have painted works well with virtually any color flower. If you're unsure what colors to use, refer back to Chapter 4, "Painting Leaves and Flowers," or look at Chapter 8, "Intermission."

I am going to use a red color scheme, without doing a silk technique. This will differentiate flowers from leaves, making them less reflective and giving them a softer look. I used rose for shading and crimson mixed with the leftover rose for the final color.

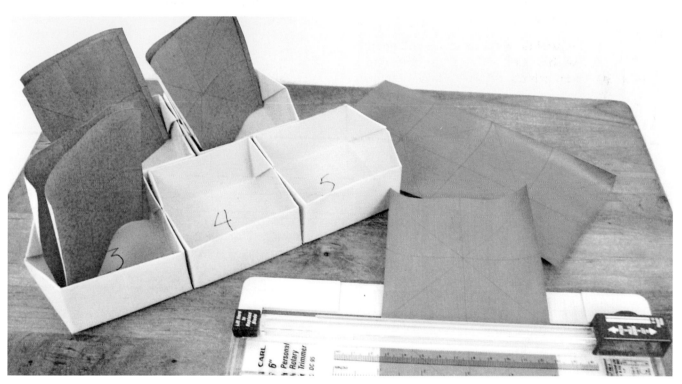

11. Cut your sheets of leaves into squares and collapse them.

12. Sharpen the folds of your collapsed leaf-squares with your wallpaper roller.

13. Fold your leaf pattern into the collapsed square, and then roll the folds with your wall paper roller.

14. Open the collapsed squares and cut them into individual leaves.

15. Store unfolded leaves in a sorting tray.

16. Partially fold flowers and use a wallpaper roller to sharpen their folds. You can pack them in a tackle box allowing you to fold them anywhere.

17. Fold all leaves and flowers.

18. Put a flower under the corresponding branch that it will be attached to.

19. Apply glue between the folds of the base of a flower and attach it to the twig.

20. Glue your first set of leaves to the twig. These should be your smallest and darkest (if you did gradient color) set of leaves. They get attached to the deepest areas of the twig. Make sure you remove the twig's bark by sanding before gluing.

These are two views of my Origami Bonsai after the first set of leaves were attached. Notice how the leaves are attached rearmost in the twig, and that they are all attached at the same angle.

21. Now glue the second largest set of leaves to the twig.

22. And then the third set of leaves.

23. Now the fourth set.

24. And finally, the fifth set.

25. Paint all leaf connections, all glued areas, and all sanded areas. Don't forget to paint the glue that holds your twig to its base.

Top: *The completed Origami Bonsai with gradient colored leaves in five sizes. Notice how the deeper leaves look darker than the ones in the front, and how light dances on the leaves, but not on the flowers. And, can you distinguish any difference in the sizes of the leaves?*

Right: *The completed sculpture viewed from the side. Notice how the leaves are aligned parallel to each other.*

CHAPTER 13

Creating Multi-Flower Assemblies

In this chapter I describe how to build multi-flower assemblies. These assemblies are important, as they are common in nature. For example, Columbine, one of my favorite flowers, is composed of a smaller group of petals in front of a larger group. Often the color of the large petals is different than the smaller. And some varieties of Columbine take colors to extremes.

I believe I have only scratched the surface when it comes to combining different variants of origami flowers. As it is quite time consuming to paint, then fold different flowers, when I have an idea for combining flowers, I always make a prototype from unpainted paper first.

An example of a Hyacinth flower assembly which is composed of eight Primrose flowers.

The Columbine

A Columbine assembly is made up of two pieces of paper, one folded in "Daisy" style (see page 73) and the other folded in the "Primrose" or "Thistle" style (see page 71 or 72). The Primrose in the center is one-quarter the size of the Daisy.

1. To make a Columbine assembly you start with two squares, one of which is one quarter the size of the other.

2. Assembly is simple. Glue a Primrose to the center of a Daisy.

This is the same assembly with an extra tier of Daisy. The back tier of Daisy is slightly larger than the front tier, making it look like they're the same size.

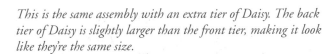

Here is another Columbine in silk-technique yellow.

The Hyacinth

The Hyacinth is made up of one large flower finished in "Daisy" style (see page 73), eight Primroses (see page 71), and a pyramid. These are time-consuming flowers to produce because their paper requirements are high. The Daisy must be painted on both sides.

Each Primrose is folded from a square one-quarter the size of the Daisy flower. The pyramid is also folded from a square one-quarter the size of the Daisy.

The Daisy and pyramid are painted on both sides in the same color as the leaf color. Primroses are painted in leaf color on one side and flower color on the other. Alignment during assembly is important.

One large square and one quarter sized square painted in leaf color along with eight squares painted in flower color create a Hyacinth assembly.

The smaller, leaf colored square is folded into a pyramid. The largest square is folded into a Daisy, and the flower colored squares are folded into Primroses.

Folding the Pyramid

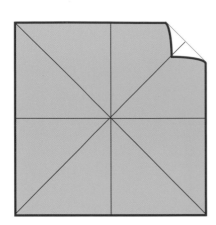

The pyramid is folded from a piece of paper one-quarter the size of the piece you use for the daisy. It can be painted on one side, or both sides.

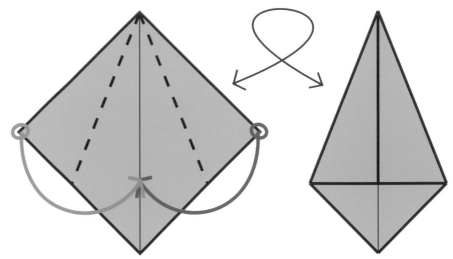

1. Start with a collapsed square (Step 5 from "Folding Impatiens" on page 24). With the open end at the top, fold each side to the center fold. Flip it and do the same on the opposite side.

2. Your model should look like this. Completely unfold it.

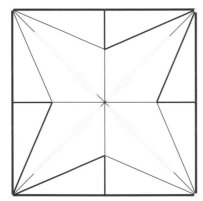

3. Reverse all folds marked in red and collapse with diagonals going to the center.

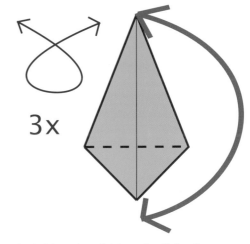

4. Fold and unfold each of the four tips as shown. You will need to flip and book-fold to complete this step.

5. Pull opposite tips to reveal a square in the center. Flatten the square, and shape into a pyramid.

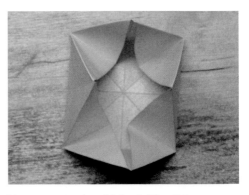

Your paper should look like this.

Assembling the Hyacinth

1. Glue the tips of the pyramid together.

2. Glue the pyramid to the Daisy, aligning the corners of the pyramid to the center folds of the Daisy.

3. Glue the first two flowers to the pyramid. Align the petals with the top of the pyramid making sure they barely touch each other.

Here's another view of the alignment of the first two flowers.

4. Glue the next two flowers between the first two.

5. Now glue your remaining four flowers on the four flat sides of the pyramid.

Note the alignment of the side flowers. Their top petal is underneath the petals of the top flowers. Your completed Hyacinth should look like this.

Fixing Mistakes

After you have completed your first Origami Bonsai, you may be bothered by the position of one of its leaves or flowers. Luckily, the glue we use is quite forgiving. It can be melted repeatedly.

In the example on the top of the opposite page, I aligned each set of leaves according to a "rule." The rule was that, for each set of leaves, the leaf closest to the branch should be attached in the direction of growth of the branch. I accidentally broke this rule when I glued the circled set of leaves. I also ran out of the largest sized leaves, leaving a gap in the lower left side of the Bonsai.

Because this is an incremental leaf Origami Bonsai, I need to put a set of the largest size leaves in the gap. Therefore, I must move the misaligned set of leaves, replacing a set of large leaves with them, and then move the large leaves to the gap.

To Remove Leaves

1. Touch a warm glue gun to the glue holding the leaves in place. Melt off the leaves you want to change.

2. Once the leaves have been removed, rub off excess glue with your fingers. Re-glue the leaves (for instructions, review Chapter 3, "Building a Basic Bonsai Assembly").

The composition before repair.

The corrected Origami Bonsai is shown here. I believe it is vastly improved. This method can also be used to remove or re-align flowers. I've even disassembled entire Origami Bonsai using this method (because I liked the branch, but not my colors).

Mistakes in Color

It's important to note that color mistakes should not be corrected with new paint after an Origami Bonsai has been assembled. Once the paper's been folded into a completed flower or leaf, adding moisture, like the water in paint, is a mistake. While you may affect the color, you'll blur the folds, and cause the paper to warp. Prior to final folding, make all the changes to color you desire.

"Franken Bonsai," depicted at right was my first attempt at a graft. The large branch in the rear that droops down was added to the main branch. It would have been a great creation except that I don't like the colors.

Sometimes color combinations work when you think you've failed. When I finished folding the leaves on this Bonsai I thought it was a failure, but after assembly I think it looks wonderful.

Depth Enhancement Errors

This piece has a different problem, which isn't apparent in this photograph. When cutting the leaves for this piece, I used too large an increment in leaf size. Instead of getting a greater three-dimensional enhancement, I just got something that looks weird. It doesn't look bad, just weird. Try to keep your increments in leaf size fairly small when you start working on depth enhancement.

Tipsy Bonsai

I often complete an Origami Bonsai only to discover that it falls over. When attaching your twig to its base, try to make sure you have accounted for all the weight you will be adding in leaves and flowers. Despite my best efforts, I often have a "tipsy" bonsai that needs a modification.

To fix the problem, I keep a set of pebbles in stock. I have numerous small clinkers and other varieties of stone to match what I'm working with. Take a small stone and glue it to your larger base-stone on the bottom of the side that the Bonsai tends to tip towards.

Above: *Glue a small pebble to stabilize tipsy bonsai.*

Left: *This image shows the direction of the tipping.*

CHAPTER

15

Housekeeping

Your Origami Bonsai works are fairly delicate. You should expect them to shed small amounts of bark over time, but generally they should age well. Because they do shed, you need to be careful when cleaning them. To remove dust, you can use a blow drier set to its lowest setting, and with its heat turned off.

Cleaning Origami Bonsai

If your Origami Bonsai gets a spatter of some sort on it, you can clean it, as long as you used artists' medium when you painted it. Simply dampen a paper towel and dab—don't rub—the spatter until it has been removed. Make sure you dusted the Origami Bonsai before you try to clean it, as dust and wet dabbing make mud, which will make matters worse.

Hanging your Origami Bonsai

I use these removable plastic stick-on hangers for all of my wall-mounted Origami Bonsai. They're nice because they come with extra double-sided stickers so you can move them.

Very small stick-on hooks can be used to hang Origami Bonsai because the pieces are not very heavy.

Storing Materials

I recycle supermarket containers to store future work, clinkers, and works in progress. Wash any container before you use it for storage with dilute soapy water, and dry them thoroughly. I also use these containers to hold smaller items, like refrigerator magnets, that are to be shipped. I pack the magnets in a small container, and then surround it with crumpled newspaper in a larger, shippable cardboard box.

Moving Origami Bonsai

One of the worst things you can do to an Origami Bonsai is put it in a car and bring it somewhere. When I have to move an Origami Bonsai I tie it into a box I've made that I poked holes in. I then loop twine around the Bonsai's trunk and through two of the holes to hold it in place during the move. I also try to find someone to open doors for me while I'm carrying the bonsai. Try to remember that an Origami Bonsai won't break on its own; failure to plan a move is all it takes to ruin it.

Shipping Origami Bonsai

I ship Origami Bonsai in a box within a box. I attach the Bonsai to the inner box using long twist ties, which can be found at gardening stores. Loop a tie around each twig. Then push the tie through two holes you make in the inner box. Twist the tie on the outside of the inner box to secure the Origami Bonsai to the inner box. Tape the inner box closed. Next, fill the bottom of the outer box with crumpled newspaper, insert the sealed inner box, and stuff crumpled newspaper around and on top of the inner box. Seal the outer box and, and label it with both "fragile" and "this side up" placards. Lastly, take it to your local shipping store and ship it with insurance, so hopefully they'll take better care when transporting it.

Safety

When I was young my father taught me how to start a campfire. We started with wads of crumpled-up paper, and put some dried twigs on top. Then we lit a match under the paper. The fire roared within a few seconds.

Origami Bonsai are made out of paper and dried twigs. That means they are extremely flammable, and all they need is a source of ignition to become roaring fires. Keep all Origami Bonsai away from any open flame or source of heat.

Keep Origami Bonsai at least three feet from:

- Candles
- Gas stoves
- Open flame
- Heaters
- Light bulbs
- Any heat-producing device

The leaves and flowers of an Origami Bonsai look delicious, and small children will want to eat them. Sadly, even though they're made from non-toxic materials, Origami Bonsai are a choking hazard. Keep all your works well out of reach of children.

While Origami Bonsai are pet-safe, pets are not Origami Bonsai-safe. Place your Origami Bonsai so that your animals cannot eat them, but if they do, panic over your bonsai, not your pet. The wood, glue, paper, and paint Origami Bonsai are made out of are non-toxic.

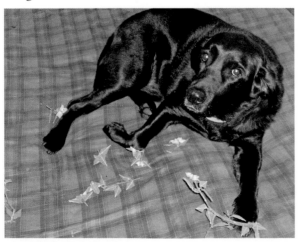

A good Origami Bonsai looks delicious to children and animals. Be sure to keep them out of reach of both.

Greater Than the Sum of Its Parts

I teach a math class called "Origami Bonsai and Fibonacci" on a voluntary basis at local public schools. I teach the students how to fold a leaf. I then leave with the student-folded leaves, use them to build an Origami Bonsai, and deliver the finished product back to the school. These bonsai hang at various schools, allowing students the experience of cooperating to build something greater than the sum of its parts. The Origami Bonsai pictured below was made by students at the Blackstone Academy in Pawtucket, Rhode Island.

I've also attended Origami Bonsai dinner parties where I've taught guests to fold leaves and assembled the host's completed bonsai after the meal. I've also been asked to host "mass foldings," where volunteers distribute leaf paper, and I demonstrate how to fold a leaf in front of the crowd. The leaves can be collected and assembled into an Origami Bonsai for the group.

A therapist friend of mine wants to use this book as part of her couples therapy program. She envisions one spouse folding while the other paints. She hopes it will be effective in improving communication and cooperation between the two.

Origami Bonsai assembled with leaves folded by students at the Blackstone Valley Academy in Pawtucket, Rhode Island, USA.

Marketing Origami Bonsai

You would think that selling a good work would be as easy as bringing it to your local art dealer. It's not. It is hard to find an art dealer who will accept works of unknown artists, even on consignment. To make matters worse, most people don't know what an Origami Bonsai is, and art dealers prefer work that is easy to sell and does not require explanation.

If your work can't be seen by the public there will never be demand for it. On that basis I have given away many of my projects in an attempt to create demand for them. I've given Origami Bonsai to various institutions and organizations, as well as to special people.

The Trump Organization has one of my works, as well as Citizens Bank, based here in Rhode Island. During the presidential campaign of 2008 I sent "First Lady Collections" of lapel pins to both Mrs. Cindy McCain and Mrs. Michelle Obama. While I hope Mrs. McCain received her pins, Mrs. Obama did not, as the package was accepted, and then shipped back to me with a label stating that they don't accept packages.

I have found the Internet to be a valuable resource for selling my work. My Origami Bonsai have been available through eBay for years, and most recently I joined Etsy and have listed many of my Origami works there.

Selling Origami Bonsai Over the Internet

To sell your work over the Internet there are a few requirements. You must have a credit card, a bank account, and you should have a computer. You will also need to set up accounts at various Internet organizations.

The first account you need to set up is at PayPal. com. PayPal is fundamentally a bank-like institution for the Internet. If someone is going to buy one of your products, they pay for it with their credit card through PayPal. Setting up a PayPal account allows you to accept payment from credit cards, debit cards, and electronic transfers. Saying you "accept PayPal" means you accept virtually any form of electronic payment.

This convenience comes with a price, however. PayPal charges two to five percent of the total amount, plus 30 cents for handling the transaction.

Once you've set up a PayPal account, and can receive payments, you can then set up an Etsy or eBay account to display and sell your creations. eBay is an Internet auction site, and Etsy is an Internet site that specializes in hand-made products. Both sites charge fees to list your products.

Etsy has a fixed-price listing schedule. You pay 20 cents per item you list for a four-month period. If the item sells, Etsy takes a 3.5 percent commission from the selling price. In other words, you're paying 20 cents to potentially make the selling price of an Origami Bonsai. To me, that's an incredible bargain, and other artists are discovering the value of this site at a rapid pace.

People post products they wish to sell on eBay for periods of one to seven days. If the product doesn't sell, it is removed from eBay's site and has to be re-posted. Charges for product postings vary based on the options chosen for the listing, and are generally more expensive than Etsy. If the product sells, eBay charges a significant commission.

At eBay there is no set price. eBay buyers determine a work's price. You can set a minimum price, and there is the potential for your work's price to be bid up.

At time of writing, eBay has a greater following than Etsy, especially among the international community. I usually make one product available on eBay to maintain a presence, while listing almost everything I make on Etsy. I've found Etsy to be so inexpensive that when people go to my web site (www.Benagami.com), if they click on "Buy Origami Bonsai," the link takes them to my page on Etsy.

One important tip, always take really good pictures of your work. Include close-ups, take your Origami Bonsai outdoors and take "action" shots. The clearer and more dramatic the pictures, the more likely your creations are to sell.

About the Author

In 2006 my life came to a turning point. I had found success in the business world, turned to teaching as a creative outlet, but something was missing. My sister had no idea at the time that the two books she sent me on advanced origami techniques would change the direction my life was going.

Origami has been a family tradition since I was a child. A colleague of my father's had published a book on origami. My father brought home his friend's book to share with our family at Christmas in 1974. I began experimenting with designs with my father and we incorporated the art of origami into our family Christmas traditions.

Life pulled me away from family and the holiday traditions, but somewhere just underneath the surface of my analytical mind there lingered a desire to recapture the creativity I had enjoyed as a child. Origami had always been attractive to me because of its paradox of complexity and simplicity. Creating with paper is a natural art; a natural art that has been a part of me since childhood.

Over the past three years Origami Bonsai has become a way of life. From a few stray folds in 2006 that created a perfectly-shaped flower from an eagle design I have built an artist's life. I have just completed another book: Advanced Origami Bonsai, and am working on Origami Bonsai Accessories. I am currently writing a magazine article entitled *Art in Zero G* that discusses art forms that can and cannot be performed by astronauts.

My revolutionary approach to the art inspires my continued creation of Origami Bonsai botanical sculptures. The beauty of Origami Bonsai is that you don't have to be a professional artist or craftsman to create intricate and beautiful botanical sculptures. With each page of this book you have the opportunity to create your own sculptures and to be an artist yourself.

I consider myself fortunate to have discovered my own creative outlet in Origami Bonsai. My life has become focused on sharing the history, beauty and simplicity of this traditional art form with others. I have found personal enrichment in developing new and revolutionary approaches to Origami Bonsai and am living a life of sharing my insights into the art with others.

— Benjamin Coleman

Joining an Art Organization

Virtually every city and town has art clubs. By joining these groups you will not only meet new people, but you will also receive invitations to participate in arts and crafts shows. I have found these groups reliable sources for information, suggestions, and creative ideas.

www.OrigamiBonsai.org

I have started a web site called OrigamiBonsai.org for Origami Bonsai artists. You can post pictures of your creations and share ideas with other people. I am hopeful that by teaching others this exciting new art form that they will take it to new heights.